Understanding How to

Put Heaven into Your Day
and

Kick Hell Out

A Handbook of
Scriptures, Affirmations and Prayers

By
Mary E. Scott Mayo

Xulon PRESS

Understanding How to Put Heaven into Your Day and Kick Hell Out
A Handbook of Scriptures, Affirmations and Prayers
by Mary E. Scott Mayo

Printed in the United States of America

ISBN 978-1-60477-075-9

www.xulonpress.com

The Lord's Prayer

Our Father which art in heaven,
Hallowed be thy name.
Thy kingdom come.
Thy will be done in earth,
as it is in heaven.
Give us this day our daily bread.
And forgive us our debts, as we
forgive our debtors.
And lead us not into temptation, but
deliver us from evil:
For thine is the kingdom, and the power,
and the glory, for ever. Amen.

St. Matthew 6:9-13

Contents

Dedication

This book is dedicated to the memory of my beloved mother, Annie Mae Johnson Scott, the one who taught me the value of righteousness. Her love for God will abide forever.

Annie Mae Johnson Scott,
a mother indeed
who won many souls to Christ
through love and wisdom.
January 30, 1928 – October 28, 2002

I also dedicate this book to the memory of my beloved sister, Sadie Irene and beloved brother, David Jerome, for their faith and love for Jesus and their belief in me.

Acknowledgments

Thanksgiving and praise to the Holy Spirit for enabling me to finish my first book. I also give special thanks to:

My husband, Clarence, for his love and support, which sustains me in the long hours spent at my desk on the computer.

My daughter, Cherry, whose ministry in songs has taken me to a new level in praise and worship.

My daughter, Candace, whose positive words and anointed ministry inspires me to reach for the stars.

My granddaughter, Jalyn, who's bright, creative, and lots of fun.

The body of Christ, Joy and Deliverance Christian Church, for their steadfast love, support, and inspiration.

My sisters: Sylvia, Tina, Lottie; brothers: Bud, Randolph, Nathan, Marshall, and Stewart for love, support, prayers and enjoying good times together.

My heritage, the Scott-Evans Family for remarkable strength, unity, and love throughout generations.

Thank you, dear readers for allowing me to share these scriptures, affirmations, and prayers with you.

Introduction

Understanding How to Put Heaven into Your Day and Kick Hell Out

Early one morning after reading the Bible, speaking positive affirmations, and doing aerobics, the Holy Spirit spoke to me. He said, ***"Put Heaven into Your Day and Kick Hell Out."*** Wow!

For four months I've been sticking with my routine. Consistently reading the Word, affirming the Word, and talking to God in prayer gave me an understanding about how to put heaven into my day.

Heaven is not automatic…You need preparation to get there. Start today by speaking Spirit-filled words to put you in heavenly places. *"And hath raised us up together, and made us sit together in heavenly places in Christ Jesus: that in the ages to come he might shew the exceeding riches of his grace in his kindness toward us through Christ Jesus" (Ephesians 2:6-7).*

Put heaven (strength, joy, peace, faith, wealth, satisfaction) into your day as you speak the scriptures, pray, and affirm the Word of God. You can be confident that you are praying in line with God's will and that He will honor His Word. Take hold of the Word and kick hell (destruction, worry, fear, confusion and torment) out. Allow God to work on your behalf as you read scriptures, speak affirmations and prayers in this book.

I will explain what the Holy Spirit revealed to me. you, too, can put heaven into your day—everyday. *"That your days may be multiplied, and the days of your children, in the land which the Lord swear unto your fathers to give them, as the days of heaven upon the earth" (Deuteronomy 11:21).* Please continue to read.

The Holy Spirit let me know that I am abounding in the God-kind of life by affirming Spirit-filled words. *"The tongue of the wise is health" (Proverbs 12:18).* Words are either positive or negative, life or death. *"Death and life are in the power of the tongue: and they that love it shall eat the fruit thereof" (Proverbs 18:21).* I am making God happy and bringing glory to Him by speaking His Word. The Word spoken out of my mouth brought life and victory throughout my day. I am able to handle every situation with ease through the Holy Spirit.

Affirming the Word of God built me up to be strong in the power of the Holy Spirit. *"A wholesome tongue is a tree of life" (Proverbs 15:4).* The Holy Spirit is sharp! He is the best teacher. He is creative and able to provide whatever we can ever ask or think. The Lord let me know that I am doing the right thing. I know in my spirit that it is—Holy Ghost Victory! The devil is defeated. Jesus is Lord. Jesus reigns forever! The Word motivates to step up to a higher way of living and having good success in life.

Keep the Word in front of you and meditate on it to make your way prosperous and to have good success. *"This book of the law shall not depart out of thy mouth; but thou shalt meditate therein day and night, that thou mayest observe to do according to all that is written therein: for then thou shalt make thy way prosperous, and then thou shalt have good success" (Joshua 1:8).*

It is clear. The Holy Spirit spoke to me and said, *"Put heaven into my day by releasing the ability of God through faith-filled words and faith actions."* Give God's Word first place in your life. Allowing His Word to be spoken out of your mouth in the beginning of your day puts heaven (peace, wisdom, understanding, confidence, joy, and overcoming power) into your day. The Word helps you treat everybody right. *"She openeth her mouth with wisdom; and in her tongue is the law of kindness" (Proverbs 31:26).*

God wants His will done on earth as it is in heaven. I enjoy saying The Lord's Prayer every day because it puts me into the faith zone. It is complete and fulfilling. The Lord's Prayer taught me how to pray. Jesus taught His disciples to pray. *"Thy will be done in earth, as it is in heaven" (St. Matthew 6:10).*

God's will is abundant life, to the full, and to the overflow. God's will is health, wealth, riches, prosperity, love, peace, faith, confidence, wisdom, knowledge, understanding and every good thing promised in His Word. God wants His will done on earth as it is in heaven. We can make it happen through the spoken Word.

Hell (destruction, worry, fear, torment and confusion) is automatically kicked out when God is first in your day. I am not excusing opposition, tests, and trials from the Christians' lives. *"When the enemy shall come in like a flood, the Spirit of the Lord shall lift up a standard against him"* (Isaiah 59:19).

My friend, put heaven into your day by laying hold of the Word of God. And not letting go until you see manifestation. The Word declares, *"If you be willing and obedient, you shall eat the good of the land"* (Isaiah 1:19). *"If they obey and serve him, they shall spend their days in prosperity, and their years in pleasures"* (Job 36:11).

There is only one way to put heaven into your day everyday, and that is through the Word of God. The Word of God delivers from the lack of health, peace, and finances. The Word is the living fountain of water that produces strength, wealth and honor. May this book be a blessing to *Understanding How to Put Heaven into Your Day and Kick Hell Out.*

Chapter 1

Absorb the Word First

*Let the word of Christ dwell in you richly in all
wisdom; teaching and admonishing one another in
psalms and hymns and spiritual songs, singing with
grace in your hearts to the Lord.*
Colossians 3:16

We need to know the mind of Christ. And what He thinks on the issues of life. The only way to find the mind of Christ is through reading and understanding the Word of God. Getting your mind absorbed in the Word is the beginning of wisdom and prosperity. The scripture says *"let the mind of Christ dwell in you richly in all wisdom."*

Absorb the Word like a sponge. When the pressures of life come upon you, release the Word out of your mouth. The Word is quick. The Word is sharp. The Word is powerful. The Word is a discerner of good and evil. *"For the word of God is quick, and powerful, and sharper than any two edged sword, piercing even to the dividing asunder of soul and spirit, and of the joints and morrow, and is a discerner of the thoughts and intents of the heart" (Hebrew 4:12).*

Submit to God. Resist the devil through speaking the Word. The devil will flee. *"Submit yourselves therefore to*

God. Resist the devil, and he will flee from you. Draw nigh to God, and he will draw nigh to you. Cleanse your hands, ye sinners; and purify your hearts, ye double minded" (James 4:7-8). Your ammunition is the Word of God. You make better choices when the Word is active in your life. The Word releases the ability of God to do His excellent greatness.

God's Word is priority for a victorious life. Everything that exists in heaven and earth is because of His Word. God created everything through His spoken Word. *"In the beginning was the Word, and the Word was with God, and the Word was God. The same was in the beginning with God. All things were made by him; and without him was not any thing made that was made" (St. John 1:1-3).*

Keep the Word in your mouth for fellowship with God. He is attentive to His Word. God acts on His spoken Word. Absorbing the Word is taking it into your heart, eyes, ears, and speaking it out through your mouth.

> *"My son, attend to my words; incline thine ear unto my sayings. Let them not depart from thine eyes; keep them in the midst of thine heart. For they are life unto those that find them, and health to all their flesh. Keep thy heart with all diligence; for out of it are the issues of life. Put away from thee a forward mouth, and perverse lips put far from thee. Let thine eyes look right on, and let thine eyelids look straight before thee. Ponder the path of thy feet, and let all thy ways be established. Turn not to the right hand nor to the left: remove thy foot from evil."*
>
> *Proverbs 4:20-27*

Psalms 119:89 says, *"For ever O Lord, thy word is settled in heaven."* What God said is already settled. God will not go back on what He said. God's supernatural power is in His spoken Word.

The power of the spoken Word will pull you out of any hole, rut, or pit. God's Word is established in heaven and will make Satan run back to his pit!

Chapter 2

Put the Word in Action

*And he shall be like a tree planted by the rivers of
water, that bringeth forth his fruit in his season; his
leaf also shall not wither; and whatsoever he doeth
shall prosper.*
Psalm 1:3

No one will be successful in life just hearing the Word.
God wants us to hear the Word and do the Word. In
other words, put the Word into action. *"But be ye doers of
the word, and not hearers only, deceiving your own selves"*
(James 1:22).

It has been in my spirit for some years now to write a
book. I have talked about writing a book for about seven
years. Some folks began to think my vision was just my
imagination. I prayed and listened to the Holy Spirit. I began
to watch to see what the Lord will say unto me. The Lord let
me know *"he becometh poor that dealeth with a slack hand:
but the hand of the diligent maketh rich" (Proverbs 10:4).*

The Lord let me know that I had to put action to my
talk. Get my hands busy with this powerful work of the Holy
Spirit. *"The Lord will prosper whatever you set your hand to
do" (Deuteronomy 28:8, 12).* Divine motivation comes from

the Lord. Passion comes from your earnest desire to fulfill the God-ordained destiny upon your life.

I have found no action is the reason for lack and poverty. The mouth talks too much. The diligent use of the brain and hands will produce success. In order to act on the principles of the Word, you may have to do a few things you don't want to do, such as deny yourself and say no to the fleshly desires. *"Then said Jesus unto his disciples, If any man will come after me, let him deny himself, and take up his cross, and follow me" (Matthew 16:24).*

Satan does not want You acting on the Word. In Mark 4:13, Jesus said that Satan came to steal the Word of God. Satan may be able to steal the Word from some people; but if You keep hearing and doing the Word, he won't be able to steal it from You! *"Faith comes by hearing, and hearing by the word of God" (Romans 10:17).* The Word of God declares *"Above all, taking the shield of faith, wherewith ye shall be able to quench all the fiery darts of the wicked" (Ephesians 6:16).*

God wants you to be alive and flow in the Spirit. The devil wants you to delay and drag your feet. Procrastination is the greatest enemy to obedience and success. Procrastination is of the devil and of the flesh. Putting things off will kill your dreams, your hope, and joy. When God gives an instruction, I have learned to act on it immediately. *"Take fast hold of instruction; let her not go: keep her; for she is thy life" (Proverbs 4:13).*

Are you ready to put action to the Word? Do whatever God has put into your heart to do. Nathan told King David, *"Go, do all that is in thine heart; for the Lord is with thee" (2 Samuel 7:3).*

Write that book, teach your favorite subject, learn to play an instrument, love a child, and visit an elderly person. Start the business that you have held in your heart for so long, learn to swim, paint that picture, write the song, and build your dream home. It is the Lord that gives you the desires of your heart. *"Delight thyself also in the Lord; and he shall give thee the desires of thine heart" (Psalm 37:4).*

Chapter 3

Prayer Changes Things From Natural to the Supernatural

*And when the day began to wear away, then came the twelve, and said unto him, Send the multitude away, that they may go into the towns and country round about, and lodge, and get victuals: for we are here in a desert place. But he said unto them, Give ye them to eat. And they said, We have no more but five loaves and two fishes; except we should go and buy meat for all this people. For they were about five thousand men. And he said to his disciples, Make them sit down by fifties in a company. And they did so, and made them all sit down. Then he took the five loaves and the two fishes **[natural]**, and looking up to heaven, he blessed them **[supernatural]**, and brake, and gave to the disciples to set before the multitude. And they did eat, and were all filled: and there was taken up of fragments that remained to them twelve baskets (St. Luke 9:12-17).*

Have faith in God. He will provide the natural and supernatural blessings. The natural is visible and touchable. The supernatural is the power of God to do the miraculous. The natural is limited. His supernatural is unlimited, more than enough and overflowing.

It was late in the evening. The crowd was 5,000. There was no place to buy food or to lodge. The disciples thought of an easy plan to get rid of the crowd. The disciples wanted to send the crowd away to find their own food and lodging. They thought that it was impossible to feed such a huge crowd.

They were in a place of lack (dessert). The only things they saw in the natural were five loaves of bread and two fishes. Jesus, the Blesser, took the five loaves and the two fishes. He looked up to heaven and blessed them. The supernatural power of God comes when you put what you have in His hands.

The supernatural occurred when Jesus blessed what they had. Thank God for what you have and bless it. Offer thanksgiving and praise to God for your family, the three bedroom house, the car, job, and everything you have. If you are satisfied with what You have, that's great. If You want more, put it in God's hands. Continue to do what you know is right. Believe to receive more than enough today. It pleases God to give you overflowing prosperity. *"Let the Lord be magnified, which has hath pleasure in the prosperity of his servant" (Psalm 35:26).*

Jesus gave the loaves of bread and fishes back to the disciples to distribute before the multitude. The people did eat and were filled. Twelve baskets of plenty were left over. Jesus fed 5,000 with five loaves of bread and two fishes. This is the supernatural power of God in manifestation! The supernatural is tangible to sight, touch, taste, and feeling. God takes the natural and turns it into the supernatural. *"There is nothing too hard for God" (Jeremiah 32:17).*

28

At the age of 35, I was divorced with two daughters. I had a temporary job and earning a very small salary. I was speaking faith and praying that this company would hire me full-time with benefits. The Personnel representative told me that they were very pleased with my work ethics and performance. However, they would not consider hiring me until after Christmas.

It was the second week in November and Thanksgiving was rapidly approaching. My rent and car note were paid. I had a lack of money for groceries and a lack of gas to put in the car for the upcoming week.

I dressed my daughters and drove downtown Raleigh to the department store to browse. After about an hour in the store, I bought the girls popcorn. And on the way out of the store, I met a member of the church. She was so happy to see me. She said, "The Missionary Circle nominated to bless your family for Thanksgiving." I received a $100.00 check and bags of groceries. We had plenty of turkey and trimmings and enough groceries to last through December. Praise the Lord for His bountiful blessings.

During the struggle of having a part-time job and no benefits, I continued to pay tithes and offerings to my local church. The same day the Personnel representative stated that they would not consider permanent employment until after Christmas, I received a call from IBM. The Human Resources Representative stated that they received my application and would like to offer full-time employment. I was hired in December 1983. They paid me well and appreciated my service. God opens doors. He will lay out a red carpet for His children to walk into the best. *"Serve the Lord with gladness: come before his presence with singing" (Psalm 100:2).*

There is no secret what God can do. What he does for others, He will do for you. *"For there is no respect of persons with God" (Romans 2:11).* I am a giver. Giving is the key to increase and abundance. *"But this I say, He which soweth bountifully shall reap also bountifully" (2 Corinthians 9:6).*

Giving connects you to the blessing plan *(Malachi 3:8-12)*. When you tithe and give, God's supernatural power goes into operation to act on Your behalf. God will open the floodgates of heaven and pour out supernatural blessings that You can taste, touch and feel.

Obedience to the voice of the Holy Spirit creates supernatural progress. Peter obeyed the instructions of Jesus and found money to settle a tax debt. Look at St. Matthew 17:27.

> *"Notwithstanding, lest we should offend them, go thou to the sea, and Cast an hook, and take up the fish that first cometh up; and when thou Hast opened his mouth, thou shalt find a piece of money: that take, and Give unto them for me and thee."*

Learn to listen and obey the voice of the Spirit. This is Your day for a supernatural breakthrough. *"Now unto him that is able to do exceeding abundantly above all that we ask or think, according to the power that worketh in us" (Ephesians 3:20).*

Chapter 4

Heaven or Hell

Our days are numbered on the earth. *"So teach us to number our days, that we may apply our hearts unto wisdom" (Psalm 90:12).* Since the Word of God let's us know that heaven is a real place, we should want to know more about heaven and how to prepare to go there.

According to The King James Version of the Holy Bible, scriptures declare **heaven** is the eternal dwelling place of our Heavenly Father, the angels, and souls of people that receive salvation. Heaven is where Christ sits on the right hand of God. *"Which he wrought in Christ, when he raised him from the dead, and set him at his own right hand in the heavenly places, Far above all principality, and power, and might, and dominion, and every name that is named, not only in this world, but also in that which is to come" (Ephesians 1:20).*

Jesus declares **heaven** is the Father's house where there are mansions. *"In my Father's house are many mansions: if it were not so, I would have told you. I go to prepare a place for you. And if I go and prepare a place for you, I will come again, and receive you unto myself; that where I am, there ye may be also" (St. John 14:2-3).*

Heaven is a place of beauty, joy, rest, peace, praising God, learning, meeting the elders and ones gone on before

(Revelation 21, 22). In heaven the streets are paved with gold, there is no need for lights, no more sickness, no more disease, no more tears, no more pain, or bills! Let's read Revelation 21:4-5:

> *"And God shall wipe away all tears from their eyes; and there shall be no more death, neither sorrow, nor crying, neither shall there be any more pain: for the former things are passed away. Behold I will make all things new."*

Although there are many scriptures about heaven, I have selected these:

Genesis 1:1   *In the beginning God created the heaven and the earth.*

Exodus 16:4   *Then said the Lord unto Moses, Behold, I will rain bread from heaven for you; and the people shall go out and gather a certain rate every day, that I may prove them, whether they will walk in my law, or no*

Deuteronomy 11:21   *That your days may be multiplied, and the days of your children, in the land which the Lord sware unto your fathers to give them, as the days of heaven upon the earth.*

Deuteronomy 33:13   *And of Joseph he said, Blessed of the Lord be his land, for the Precious things of heaven, for the dew, and for the deep that coucheth beneath.*

II Kings 2:11

And it came to pass, as they still went on, and talked, that, behold, there appeared a chariot of fire, and horses of fire, and parted them both asunder; and Elijah went up by a whirlwind into heaven.

II Chronicles 7:14

If my people, which are called by my name, shall humble themselves, and pray, and seek my face, and turn from their wicked ways; then will I hear from heaven, and will forgive their sin, and will heal their land.

Psalm 69:34

Let the heaven and earth praise him, the seas, and every thing that moveth therein.

Psalm 139:8

If I ascend up into heaven, thou art there: if I make my bed in hell, behold, thou art there

Daniel 2:28

But there is a God in heaven that revealeth secrets, and maketh known to the king Nebuchadnezzar what shall be in the latter days.

Malachi 3:10

Bring tithes and offerings . . .if I will not open you the windows of heaven

Matthew 3:17

And lo a voice from heaven, saying, This is my beloved Son, in whom I am well pleased.

Matthew 5:12	*Rejoice, and be exceeding glad: for great is your reward in heaven*
Matthew 6:20	*But lay up for yourselves treasures in heaven*
Acts 1:10	*And while they looked stedfastly toward heaven as he went up behold, two men stood by them in white apparel*
Revelation 21:10	*And he carried me away in the spirit to a great and high mountain, and shewed me that great city, the holy Jerusalem, descending out of heaven from God.*

Choose heaven or hell. We can choose heaven by accepting the Lord Jesus. *"That if thou shalt confess with thy mouth the Lord Jesus, and shalt believe in thine heart that God hath raised him from the dead, thou shalt be saved. For with the heart man believeth unto righteousness; and with the mouth confession is made unto salvation. For the scripture saith, Whosoever believeth on him shall not be ashamed" (Read Romans 10:9-13).*

Have no part of hell. Do not curse and tell anyone *to go to hell!* That is bad language; ugly and idle talk. I would not want my worse enemy to go to hell. No one should go to that dreadful place. Satan is doomed for hell (Revelation 20:1-3). The wicked spirit of Satan and the Devil want to deceive minds to think that there is no hell. There is a hell. The Word of God says so.

Look at these scriptures on hell.

Deuteronomy 32:22	*For a fire is kindled in mine anger, and shall burn unto the lowest hell, and shall consume the earth with her increase, and set on fire the foundations of the mountains.*
Psalm 9:17	*The wicked shall be turned into hell, and all the nations that forget God.*
Psalm 55:15	*Let death seize upon them, and let them go down quick into hell: for wickedness is in their dwellings, and among them.*
Proverbs 7:27	*Her house is the way to hell, going down to the chambers of death.*
Proverbs 15:11	*Hell and destruction are before the Lord: how much more then the hearts of the children of men?*
Proverbs 15:24	*The way of life is above to the wise, that he may depart from hell beneath.*
Proverbs 27:20	*Hell and destruction are never full; so the eyes of man are never satisfied.*
Matthew 16:18	*And I say also unto thee, That thou art Peter, and upon this rock I will build my church; and the gates of hell shall not prevail against it.*
Matthew 23:33	*Ye serpents, ye generation of vipers, how can ye escape the damnation of hell?*

Acts 2:31

> He seeing this before spake of the resurrection of Christ, that his soul was not left in hell, neither his flesh did see corruption.

James 3:6

> And the tongue is a fire, a world of iniquity, . .is set on the fire of hell.

Revelation 20:13-14

> And the sea gave up the dead which were in it; and death and hell delivered up the dead which were in them: and they were judged every man according to their works. And death and hell were cast into the lake of fire. This is the second death.

The Lord is loving and kind to all of us. He made us for His glory. Today, make a decision to choose heaven by the life you live and the work you do. *"And, behold, I come quickly; and my reward is with me, to give every man according as his work shall be" (Revelation 22:12).*

Chapter 5

Scriptures * Affirmations * Prayers

Abide

But the anointing which ye have received of him abideth in you, and ye need not that any man teach you: but as the same anointing teacheth you of all things, and is truth, and is no lie, and even as it hath taught you, ye shall abide in him. And now, little children, abide in him; that, when he shall appear, we may have confidence, and not be ashamed before him at his coming.

I John 2:27- 28

Affirmation:
The Holy Spirit abides in me and teaches me all things.

Prayer:

Father, I know that I am not alone. Your Spirit abides in me. Thank You for walking and talking with me. I thank You for teaching me to take rest and comfort in Your Word. You are my confidence and joy. I thank You for Your presence and love. In the name of Jesus, amen.

Anointing (The)

And it shall come to pass in that day, that his burden shall be taken away from off thy shoulder, and his yoke from off thy neck, and the yoke shall be destroyed because of the anointing.

Isaiah 10:27

Affirmation:
I have the burden-removing, yoke-destroying power
of God in my life.

Prayer:
Father, in the name of Jesus, I confess that the burden has been taken away and off my shoulders. I refuse to be bowed down with the cares of this world. I release my faith and let go of every negative thought. I claim salvation, healing, and deliverance in the name of Jesus. Amen.

Appetite

All the labour of man is for his mouth, and yet the appetite is not filled.

Ecclesiastes 6:7

Affirmation:
The Lord is my satisfaction.

Prayer:

Father, in the name of Jesus, I praise You for delivering me from the spirit of defeat and insecurity. I elevate my mind to think on those things that are true, honest, just, pure, lovely, and of good report. The past mistakes will not lord over me. I renew my mind to fresh thoughts of peace and joy in the Holy Spirit. Father, I thank You for grace and peace in Jesus' name. Hallelujah!

Authority

Behold, I give unto You power to tread on serpents and scorpions, and over all the power of the enemy: and nothing shall by any means hurt You.

Luke 10:19

Affirmation:
God has given me power over the enemy.

Prayer:
Father, You are the power abiding in me to overthrow every wicked spirit of the enemy. You said in Your Word that nothing shall hurt me. Satan, I resist every oppressive spirit in the name of Jesus. I resist fear, discouragement, and depression. I speak the Word of truth, in the power of God, and I give no place to Satan. Thank You, Father, in Jesus' name that I am set free from every wicked spirit. Amen.

Believe

And they said, believe on the Lord Jesus Christ, and thou shalt be saved, and thy house.

Acts 16:31

Affirmation:
Jesus is my Saviour.

Prayer:

Father, in the name of Jesus, Your Word said that if I confess with my mouth the Lord Jesus, and believe in my heart that God has raised Him from the dead, I shall be saved. For with the heart, man believeth unto righteousness and with the mouth, confession is made unto salvation. I believe in my heart and confess with my mouth that Jesus is Lord. Thank You for salvation. I have a new life in Christ. Praise the Lord!

Beauty

He hath made every thing beautiful in his time: also he hath set the world in their heart, so that no man can find out the work that God maketh from the beginning to the end.

Ecclesiastes 3:11

Affirmation:
God made me beautiful.

Prayer:

Father, in the name of Jesus, I pray that Your beauty will radiate through me to bring salvation to many. Thank You, Father, for beautifying me with Your salvation in Jesus' name. Amen.

Build

But ye, beloved, building up yourselves on Your most holy faith, praying in the Holy Ghost, keep yourselves in the love of God, looking for the mercy of our Lord Jesus Christ unto eternal life.

Jude 1:20-21

Affirmation:
My faith is built on Jesus Christ.

Prayer:

Father, in the name of Jesus, I thank You for building up my faith by praying in the Holy Ghost. I throw off everything that is not like You. I put on Your love and mercy through Jesus Christ I pray. Amen.

Business

Seest thou a man diligent in his business? He shall stand before kings; he shall not stand before mean men.

Proverbs 22:29

Affirmation:
Diligent in business is my door to greatness.

Prayer:

Father, in the name of Jesus, I pray and confess that the Holy Spirit will empower me to do exceedingly well in business. I ask for creativity and insight in marketing products that will yield a great profit. Father, I give thanks for capital, resources, and the right people to be successful. Jesus is Lord! Amen.

Cares

Casting all Your care upon him; for he careth for You.

I Peter 5:7

Affirmation:
The Lord cares for me.

Prayer:

Father, You said to cast my burden upon the Lord, and He shall sustain me: He shall never suffer the righteous to be moved. I honor Your Word. Therefore, I refuse to carry the burdens and cares of this life. I cast them upon You forever. I give You the praise for the victory is mine in Jesus name. Amen.

Children

Ye are of God, little children, and have overcome them: because greater is he that is in You, than he that is in the world.

I John 4:4

Affirmation:
My children are winners and overcomers.

Prayer:
Father, in the name of Jesus, I pray and confess Your Word over my children that You will build a hedge of protection around them. I confess that my children choose life and life more abundantly. I confess that my children honor their parents that it will be well, and they live long and prosperous on the earth. Therefore, my children are highly favored with God and man. Thank You, Father, in Jesus' name that they are free from every evil work. I give You praise for it all, Father, in the name of Jesus. Amen.

Confidence

And this is the confidence that we have in him, that, if
we ask any thing according to his will, he heareth us:
And if we know that he hear us, whatsoever we ask,
we know that we have the petitions that we desired
of him.

I John 5:14-15

Affirmation:
My confidence is in the Lord.

Prayer:
Father, in the name of Jesus, my confidence is in Your
Word. I confess and believe that God is able to make all
grace abound toward me; that I will always have all suffi-
ciency in all things. I shall lack nothing. There is no shortage
in my life. I have more than enough to bless my family and
folks in need. God is my Source, Provider, and Creator. My
broke days are over. I am abundantly blessed. Praise the
Lord! Amen.

Consolation

Now our Lord Jesus Christ himself, and God, even our Father, which hath loved us, and hath given us everlasting consolation and good hope through grace, comfort Your hearts, and stablish You in every good word and work.

II Thessalonians 2:16-17

Affirmation:
My consolation is in Christ.

Prayer:
Dear Lord, You bore my grief, carried my sorrows and pains. I know that in the midst of hurt, You love me and will heal my wounds. Thank You for comforting my heart and establishing every good word and work. In Jesus name I pray. Amen.

Continue

If ye continue in my word, then are ye my disciples indeed; and ye shall know the truth, and the truth shall make You free.

St. John 8:31-32

Affirmation:
I know the truth and it has made me free.

Prayer:
Dear Father, in the name of Jesus, I come against every lying spirit. I bind sickness, disease, and poverty. I loose vitality, health, and wealth into my life. I believe Your Word regardless of my circumstances. Your Word says greater is He that is in me than he that is in the world. I will continue to believe Your Word because Your Word gives me life and liberty. I thank You, Father, in Jesus' name. Amen.

Death

And God shall wipe away all tears from their eyes;
and there shall be no more death, neither sorrow, nor
crying, neither shall there be any more pain: for the
former things are passed away.

Revelation 21:4

Affirmation:
God cares about me.
He wipes away my tears.

Prayer:
Our Father which art in heaven, Hallowed be thy name.
Thy kingdom come. Thy will be done in earth, as it is in
heaven. Give us this day our daily bread. And forgive us our
debts, as we forgive our debtors. And lead us not into temptation, but deliver us from evil: for thine is the kingdom, and
the power, and the glory, for ever. Amen.

Desires

Delight thyself also in the Lord; and he shall give thee the desires of thine heart. Commit thy way unto the Lord; trust also in him; and he shall bring it to pass.

Psalm 37:5-6

Affirmation:
Because I delight myself in the Lord, He gives me the desires of my heart.

Prayer:

Father, in the name of Jesus, I bring our country, our nation, and our world before You. I am concerned about the world that we live in. I am concerned about mothers, fathers, boys and girls. You said in Your Word, for God so loved the world that He gave His only begotten Son, that whosoever believeth in Him shall not perish, but shall have everlasting life. Through humility and prayer, I ask salvation and healing for the world and for Your people. I trust You Father. I thank You for answering prayer in the name of Jesus. Amen.

Diligent

He becometh poor that dealeth with a slack hand: but the hand of the diligent maketh rich.

Proverbs 10:4

Affirmation:
My hands are diligent and I am rich.

Prayer:
Father, I depart from a lazy and undisciplined lifestyle. I seek, inquire for, and pursue diligence in all that I put my hands to do. Diligence makes me rich in the Spirit, mental, physical, and financial arena. Lord, I confess and believe that the hand of the diligent shall bear rule. Thank You for igniting the spirit of diligence in me to be abundantly rich in all that I set my hands to do. I pray in the name of Jesus. Amen.

Dreams

As for these four children, God gave them knowledge and skill in all learning and wisdom: and Daniel had understanding in all visions and dreams.

Daniel 1:17

Affirmation:
I am enjoying the best.

Prayer:
Father, in the name of Jesus, when the enemy tried to stop my dreams from coming true, I persevered in faith. I confess and believe that prosperity is God's will for me and that I will not settle for less. I confess and believe that God is increasing my greatness and comforting me on every side. I am righteous and confess that wealth and riches shall be in my house and my righteousness endures for ever. I will greatly praise the Lord with my mouth and praise Him among the people for making my dreams reality. I pray in the name of Jesus. Amen.

Faith

Looking unto Jesus the author and finisher of our faith; who for the joy that was set before him endured the cross, despising the shame, and is set down at the right hand of the throne of God.

Hebrews 12:2

Affirmation:
Jesus is the author and finisher of my faith.

Prayer:
Father, in the name of Jesus, I look to You for everything that concerns me because You made me and know who I am. I confess and believe that I am wonderfully and fearfully made in Your image. I confess and believe that You have made us kings and priest unto God and His Father. To Him be glory and dominion for ever and ever. Amen.

Family

Of whom the whole family in heaven and earth is named, that he would grant You, according to the riches of his glory, to be strengthened with might by his Spirit in the inner man.

Ephesians 3:15-16

Affirmation:
My family is great in the Lord.

Prayer:
Father, as a believer, I declare and decree, "As for me and my house, we shall serve the Lord." I acknowledge and welcome the presence of Your Holy Spirit here in my family and home. I declare on the authority of Your Word that my family will be mighty in the land; this generation of the upright shall be blessed. Father, You delight in wealth and riches in our home. Your righteousness endures forever. I pray in the name of Jesus. Amen.

Favor

And Jesus increased in wisdom and stature, and in favour with God and man.

St. Luke 2:52

Affirmation:
I have favor with God and man.

Prayer:

Father, in the name of Jesus, Your wisdom causes my face to shine. I confess and believe that Your promotion causes me to ride upon the high places of the earth. Your favor produces sweat-less victory. Your favor gives me the advantage in being the "head and not the tail, first and not last, above and not beneath." Father, I thank You for giving me the wisdom to know that it is because of Your favor that life is so good! Praise the Lord!

Fear

For God hath not given us the spirit of fear; but of power, and of love, and of a sound mind.

II Timothy 1:7

Affirmation:
I have the spirit of power, love, and a sound mind.

Prayer:
Father, You have delivered me from the spirit of fear. I am no longer bound. I have been set free. Thank You for Your many blessings. In Jesus' name, amen.

Fellowship

If we say that we have fellowship with him, and walk in darkness, we lie, and do not the truth: But if we walk in the light, as he is in the light, we have fellowship one with another and the blood of Jesus Christ his Son cleanseth us from all sin.

I John 1:6-7

Affirmation:
I walk in the light and have fellowship with my sister and brother.

Prayer:

Dear Father God, I value the wonderful fellowship of Your presence and love. Thank You for being the Light that shines in my soul. Father, I pray that my light will shine so that men will see Your good works and glorify You in the name of Jesus. Amen.

Fruit

But the fruit of the Spirit is love, joy, peace, long-suffering, gentleness, goodness, faith, meekness, temperance: against such there is no law.

Galatians 5:22

Affirmation:
I live in the fruit of the Spirit.

Prayer:
Father, in the name of Jesus, I thank You for the fruit of the Spirit and Your divine empowerment. Father, forever produce Your fruit in my life that people will be inspired to taste and see that the Lord is good to all that call upon Him in the name of Jesus. Amen.

Grace

Grace be to You and peace from God the Father, and from our Lord Jesus Christ, Who gave himself for our sins, that he might deliver us from this present evil world, according to the will of God and our Father: to whom be glory for ever and ever. Amen.

Galatians 1:3-5

Affirmation:
My life is full of God's grace and peace.

Prayer:
Father, I thank You for Your grace and peace in my daily walk. I praise You for delivering me from confusion and every evil in Jesus' name. Amen.

Healing

Who his own self bare our sins in his own body on the tree, that we, being dead to sins, should live unto righteousness: by whose stripes ye were healed.

I Peter 2:24; Isaiah 53:4,5

Affirmation:

I am healed by the stripes of Jesus.

Prayer:

Father, in the name of Jesus, "surely You have borne our grieves, and carried our sorrows. You were wounded for our transgressions and bruised for our iniquities: the chastisement of our peace was upon Him; and with His stripes I am healed." I confess and believe that I am healed from the top of my head to the bottom of my feet, and all around. I thank You for my healing in the name of Jesus. Amen.

Health

Beloved, I wish above all things that thou mayest prosper and be in health, even as thy soul prospereth.

III John 1:2

Affirmation:
I am in excellent health.

Prayer:

Father, in the name of Jesus, I thank You for the best of health. I confess that the Word of God preserves me in soundness of mind, wholeness of body, and spirit. Your Word is medicine and life to my flesh. I confess that the Spirit of life operates in me and makes me free from the law of sin and death. Lord, thank You for blessing my bread and water; and fulfilling the number of my days in the name of Jesus. Amen.

Heaven

Behold, I give unto You power to tread on serpents and scorpions, and over all the power of the enemy: and nothing shall by any means hurt You. Notwithstanding in this rejoice not, that the spirits are subject unto You; but rather rejoice, because Your names are written in heaven.

Luke 10:19-20

Affirmation:
I am rejoicing that my name is written in heaven.

Prayer:
Father, in the name of Jesus, I thank You for the promise of heaven where we will see You face to face. But until then, I appreciate Your presence and guidance. Thank You for loving me; and one day welcoming me home in the name of Jesus. Amen.

Holy Ghost

But the Comforter, which is the Holy Ghost, whom the Father will send in my name, he shall teach You all things, and bring all things to Your remembrance, whatsoever I have said unto You.

St. John 14:26

Affirmation:
The Holy Ghost is my Comforter.

Prayer:
Father, in the name of Jesus, I pray that I be filled with full and clear understanding of Your will in my life. I pray to be fully pleasing to You; bearing fruit in every good work, and continually growing and increasing in Your wisdom, knowledge, and understanding. Father, I thank You for the Holy Ghost teaching me all things in the name of Jesus. Amen.

Incarcerated

But the angel of the Lord by night opened the prison doors, and brought them forth, and said, Go, stand and speak in the temple to the people all the words of this life.

The Acts 5:19-20

Affirmation:
The Gospel opens prison doors.

Prayer:
Father, in the name of Jesus, we thank You for the Holy Spirit Who shows truth to sinners and convicting them of sin, righteousness, and judgment. We release Your mercy, Your grace, and Your love to those with prison walls that they might be saved through faith. Thank You for setting the captives free. I pray in the precious name of Jesus. Amen.

Laughter

Then was our mouth filled with laughter, and our tongue with singing; then said they among the heathen, the Lord hath done great things for them. The Lord hath done great things for us; whereof we are glad.

Psalm 126:2-3

Affirmation:
The Lord fills my mouth with laughter and singing.

Prayer:
Father, this is the day the Lord has made. I rejoice. I am glad in it! The Lord is doing great things for me. My spirit rejoices. Laughter is my heritage. I am free from bondage and cares. For where the Spirit of the Lord is, there is liberty. This joy that I have the world didn't give it to me, and the world can't take it away. I abide in the kingdom of God and have peace and joy in the Holy Spirit! Praise the Lord!

Light

The Lord is my light and my salvation; whom shall
I fear? The Lord is the strength of my life; of whom
shall I be afraid?

Psalm 27:1

Affirmation:
The Lord is my light and salvation.

Prayer:

Father, God, I am Your child. I am dwelling in the secret
place of the Most High and abiding under the shadow of
the Almighty. No evil shall befall me nor shall any plague
come near me. Thank You for being the strength of my life
in Jesus' name. Amen.

Long Life

With long life will I satisfy him, and shew him my salvation.

Psalm 91:16

Affirmation:
I live a long, strong, and satisfying life.

Prayer:
Father, in the name of Jesus, I confess Your Word over my life. As I do this, I believe and say that Your Word will not return to You void, but will accomplish what it says it will. Therefore, I believe in the name of Jesus that I live a long, healthy, strong and prosperous life. I hold fast to my confession of faith in Your Word. I stand fixed and immovable in Your salvation in the name of Jesus. Amen.

Love

Beloved, if God so loved us, we ought also to love one another. No man hath seen God at any time. If we love one another, God dwelleth in us, and his love is perfected in us.

I John 4:11-12

Affirmation:
God's love dwells in me.

Prayer:

Father, I thank You for loving me. Produce in my life the God-kind of love that You speak about in I John 4:11 in Jesus' name. Amen.

Meditation

Let the words of my mouth, and the meditation of my heart, be acceptable in thy sight, O Lord, my strength, and my redeemer.

Psalm 19:14

Affirmation:
The Lord is my Redeemer.

Prayer:
Father, in the name of Jesus, Your Word declares that if I keep my mind stayed on You that You will keep me in perfect peace because I trust in You. I confess to meditate on Your Word, observe, and do accordingly. Then, I shall make my way prosperous and shall have good success. Your Word is healing to my flesh. It is prosperity to me. I rest in You. I praise You that the joy of the Lord is my strength and stronghold! In the name of Jesus I pray. Amen.

Money

A feast is made for laughter, and wine maketh merry:
but money answereth all things.

Ecclesiastes 10:19

Affirmation:
Money comes to me in Jesus' name.

Prayer:
Father, in Jesus name, Your Word declares that the earth
is the Lord's and the fullness thereof. Your Word says give,
and it shall be given unto You; good measure, pressed down,
and shaken together, and running over shall men give unto
Your bosom. I am a giver. I believe and confess that my
broke days are over! I shall never be broke again in my life!
All my needs and the desires of my heart are abundantly met
in the name of Jesus. Amen.

Overcome

And they overcame him by the blood of the Lamb, and by the word of their testimony; and they loved not their lives unto the death.

Revelation 12:11

Affirmation:
I am a winner and an over comer.

Prayer:

Father, in the name of Jesus, I am of good courage; I pray that You grant me to speak forth Your Word with authority. I am not intimidated by the enemy for I have overcame him by Your blood and by the word of my testimony. I am courageous as a lion for I have been made the righteousness of God in Christ Jesus. I am complete in Him. Praise the name of Jesus!

Peace

And the peace of God, which passeth all understanding, shall keep Your hearts and minds through Christ Jesus.

Philippians 4:7

Affirmation:
The peace of God keeps my heart and mind through Christ Jesus.

Prayer:

Father, God, You are the Prince of Peace. Your peace passes all understanding. I refuse to entertain worry and anxiety. Your Word says though I walk through the valley of the shadow of death, I will fear no evil: for thou art with me; thy rod and thy staff they comfort me. I dismiss worry and anxiety in Jesus name. I claim the peace of God that passes all understanding. Thank You Jesus! Amen.

Prayer

For the eyes of the Lord are over the righteous, and his ears are open unto their prayers: but the face of the Lord is against them that do evil.

I Peter 3:12

Affirmation:
God answers my prayer.

Prayer:

Dear Heavenly Father, thank You for hearing our prayers and watching over us. You are our constant friend and companion. Help us to keep our heart, ears and eyes open to do Your will in Jesus' name. Amen.

Promise

The Lord is not slack concerning his promise, as some men count slackness; but is longsuffering to us-ward, not willing that any should perish, but that all should come to repentance.

II Peter 3:9

Affirmation:
God is a promise keeper.

Prayer:

Lord, I recognize that You are the giver of every good and perfect gift. Help me to wait on Your time. For I know the promise may tarry but You are faithful in bringing it to pass. I thank You. Amen.

Prosper

Beloved, I wish above all things that thou mayest prosper and be in health, even as thy soul prospereth.

III John 1:1

Affirmation:
I have a prosperous spirit, soul, and body.

Prayer:

Dear Father, You are the giver of every good and perfect gift. I thank You for prospering my spirit, soul, physical, relationships, and finances in Jesus' name. Amen.

Prosperity

Let them shout for joy, and be glad that favour my righteous cause: yea, let them say continually, let the Lord be magnified, which hath pleasure in the prosperity of his servant.

Psalm 35:27

Affirmation:
I am in prosperity overflow.

Prayer:
Father, how I praise You for taking pleasure in my prosperity. You have given me the power to get wealth. I stand on Your Word. I confess and believe today is my day of promotion and breakthrough. Great things come from You, O Lord. Thank You for blessing me far above my expectations. Praise Your Holy name!

Redeem

Looking for that blessed hope, and the glorious appearing of the great God and our Saviour Jesus Christ; who gave himself for us, that he might redeem us from all iniquity, and purify unto himself a peculiar people, zealous of good works.

Titus 2:13-14

Affirmation:
I am redeemed.

Prayer:
Father, I thank You for that blessed hope. I am looking for the glorious appearing of Jesus Christ who gave himself for me. Thank You for loving me and redeeming me from all iniquity. I submit to Your will in performing good works in Jesus name, amen.

Rejoice

Rejoice in the Lord always: and again I say, Rejoice.

Philippians 4:4

Affirmation:
This is my day. I shall rejoice.

Prayer:
Father, Your Word says that the joy of the Lord is my strength. I rejoice today for You have never left me nor forsaken me. You are with me always. You have been with me in good times and bad times. You have been with me in sorrow and gladness. Your love is the same. Thank You for being the same yesterday, today, and forevermore in Jesus' name, amen.

Repent

Repent ye therefore, and be converted, that Your sins may be blotted out, when the times of refreshing shall come from the presence of the Lord.

Acts 3:19-22

Affirmation:
I am converted and my sins have been blotted out.

Prayer:

Father, in the name of Jesus and according to Your Word, I repent and ask for forgiveness of my sins. I believe my sins are blotted out. I make You Lord of my life. I confess that I have been changed by Your power and love. I am refreshed by Your Word and presence. Thank You for all Your many blessings upon my life in the name of Jesus, amen.

Request

Be careful for nothing; but in every thing by prayer and supplication with thanksgiving let Your requests be made known unto God.

Philippians 4:6

Affirmation:
My request is granted.

Prayer:

Father, in Jesus name, Your Word says not to fret. Make my requests known unto God. I pray that all of my needs and the needs of my loved ones are met spiritually, mentally, physically, socially, and financially, according to Philippians 4:19. Thank You Father. I believe it is done in Jesus name, amen.

Rest

There remaineth therefore a rest to the people of God.
For he that is entered into his rest, he also hath ceased
from his own works, as God did from his.

Hebrews 4:9-10

Affirmation:
I will rest in the Lord.

Prayer:

Father, forgive me for worrying about family, work,
finances, and people. I cast all my cares upon You. I refuse
to worry anymore. I enter Your rest by the help of the Holy
Spirit. In Jesus' name I pray. Amen.

Salvation

That if thou shalt confess with thy mouth the Lord Jesus, and shalt believe in thine heart that God hath raised him from the dead, thou shalt be saved. For with the heart man believeth unto righteousness; and with the mouth confession is made unto salvation. For the scripture saith, whosoever believeth on him shall not be ashamed. For whosoever shall call upon the name of the Lord shall be saved.

Romans 10: 9-11,13

Affirmation:
I believe with my heart and confess with my mouth that I am saved.

Prayer:
Father, in the name of Jesus, I thank You for the plan of salvation. It is Your will that all men be saved and know Your Word. Satan, I bind You in the name of Jesus and loose You from operating in the life of people who do not know Christ. I intercede for the lost and confess that they receive salvation and be filled with the Holy Spirit. Amen. It is done!

School

Wherefore the law was our schoolmaster to bring us
unto Christ, that we might be justified by faith.

Galatians 3:24

Affirmation:
Jesus is Lord over our schools.

Prayer:
Father, in the name of Jesus, I pray that You watch over
the schools. I pray that You watch over the men and women
in positions of authority within the school systems. I pray
and confess that men and women of integrity maintain these
positions. I ask that the wicked be cut off. Father, I pray that
our children will learn knowledge and skills in a wholesome
and safe environment. Thank You, Father for covering our
children with Your protection and favor today. I believe it is
done now in the name of Jesus. Amen.

Sickness

And Jesus went about all the cities and villages, teaching in their synagogues, and preaching the gospel of the kingdom, and healing every sickness and every disease among the people.

St. Matthew 9:35

Affirmation:
I am healed by the stripes of Jesus Christ.

Prayer:
Heavenly Father, in the name of Jesus, Your Word declares that by Your stripes I am healed. I stand on Your Word and proclaim my healing. Therefore, I rebuke sickness, disease and pain. These afflictions will not lord over my body. I confess that I am healed and walk in excellent health. In the name of Jesus I pray. Amen.

Sorrow

But I would not have You to be ignorant, brethren, concerning them which are asleep, that ye sorrow not even as others which have no hope. For if we believe that Jesus died and rose again, even so them also which sleep in Jesus will God bring with him.

I Thessalonians 4:13-14

Affirmation:
Lord, I believe.

Prayer:

Father, I thank You for the Holy Spirit is my Comforter, Strengthener and Teacher. Your Word declares "let not Your heart be troubled,"(John 14:1). I confess and believe that You love and care about me and will see me through to victory. Thank You for comforting my heart and wiping away my tears in the name of Jesus, amen.

Strength

I will love thee, O Lord, my strength. The Lord is my rock, and my fortress, and my deliverer; my God, my strength, in whom I will trust; my buckler, and the horn or my salvation, and my high tower.

Psalm 18:1-2

Affirmation:
The Lord is my strength.

Prayer:

Father, You see my hurts and disappointments. I pray that You strengthen me according to Your Word. I take Your Word and use it as medicine. Your Word comforts my heart and eases my pain. My help and strength comes from You, and my Youth is renewed like the eagles'. I confess and believe that this is the best day of my life because Jesus is Lord!

Success

This book of the law shall not depart out of thy mouth; but thou shalt meditate therein day and night, that thou mayest observe to do according to all that is written therein: for then thou shalt make thy way prosperous, and then thou shalt have good success.

Joshua 1:8

Affirmation:
I have good success.

Prayer:
Father, Your Word gives me life and blessed assurance. I believe and confess that I am prosperous and have good success because I meditate and act out on Your Word. Father, I thank You for blessing me with joy and good success in the name of Jesus. Amen.

Temptation

No temptation has overtaken You that is not common to man. God is faithful, and He will not let You be tempted beyond Your strength, but with the temptation will also provide the way of escape, that You may be able to endure it.

I Corinthians 10:13

Affirmation:
God is faithful.

Prayer:
Heavenly Father, temptation is on every side. I put my trust in You that in time of temptation, I will overcome by Your inner strength. Father, thank You for being faithful to Your Word. You will not allow me to be tempted more than I am able to stand. In the time of temptation, You provide a way of escape. I believe and confess that I am an overcomer in the name of Jesus. Amen.

Trouble

Who comforteth us in all our tribulation, that we may
be able to comfort them which are in any trouble, by
the comfort wherewith we ourselves are comforted
of God.

2 Corinthians 1:4

Affirmation:
God is my peace in troubled times.

Prayer:
My heavenly Father, in the name of Jesus, I am of good
courage because You are my comfort and peace in the times
of trouble. I take Your Word and confidently say, "The Lord
is my Deliverer, I will not fear or be afraid. What can man do
to me?" I boldly say, "Satan, You are defeated, for my God
and Jesus reign!" Praise the name of Jesus!

Wealth

Praise ye the Lord, blessed is the man that feareth the Lord, that delighteth greatly in his commandments. Wealth and riches shall be in his house: and his righteousness endureth forever.

Psalm 112:1,3

Affirmation:
Great wealth and riches are in my house.

Prayer:
Father, I am a giver of tithes and offerings. I confess and believe that You are bringing me into my wealthy place right now. I confess that I am debt free. I shall never be broke again another day in my life. My broke days are over! I am abundantly wealthy. Everything that I put my hands to do prospers in the name of Jesus. Amen.

Weight Control

Wherefore seeing we also are compassed about with so great a cloud of witnesses, let us lay aside every weight, and the sin which doth so easily beset us, and let us run with patience the race that is set before us.

Hebrews 12:1

Affirmation:
I have power to resist whatever is not good for me.

Prayer:
Heavenly Father, I am overweight. I ask You to rescue me from the cares and worries of life. Help me to abandon the habit of eating junk foods. I desire to eat the right portions of nutritious foods. I confess and believe to develop and maintain a consistent lifestyle of eating healthy and exercising daily. I take charge of my life in the name of Jesus. Amen.

Wisdom

If any man lack wisdom, let him ask of God, that giveth to all men liberally, and upbraideth not; and it shall be given him.

James 1:5

Affirmation:
The wisdom of God guides me to victory.

Prayer:

Father, Your Word is wisdom. Your wisdom gives me everything that pertains to life and godliness. I confess the spirit of wisdom and revelation in the knowledge of Christ. I thank You for wisdom, knowledge and understanding to do well in life. I thank You for being filled with the Spirit. In Jesus' name, amen.

Youth

Who satisfieth thy mouth with good things; so that
thy Youth is renewed like the eagle's.

Psalm 103:5

Affirmation:
The Lord renews my Youth like the eagles.

Prayer:

Father, Your Word says Moses was an hundred and
twenty years old when he died. His eye was not dim, nor his
natural force abated according to Deuteronomy 34:7. I pray
and confess that You keep my eyes, bones, and total body in
perfect health as I do my part. Thank You for all Your blessings in Jesus name. Amen.

Chapter 6

Selected Prayers from the Bible

The Prayer of Jabez

I Chronicles 4:10

And Jabez called on the God of Israel, saying,
Oh that thou wouldest bless me indeed, and enlarge
my coast, and that thine hand might be with me,
and that thou wouldest keep me from evil, that it
may not grieve me!
And God granted him that which he requested.

The Prayer of Hannah

I Samuel 2:1-11

And Hannah prayed, and said,

My heart rejoiceth in the Lord, mine horn is exalted in the Lord: my mouth is enlarged over mine enemies; because I rejoice in thy salvation.

There is none holy as the Lord: for there is none beside thee: neither is there any rock like our God.

Talk no more so exceeding proudly; let not arrogancy come out of Your mouth: for the Lord is a God of knowledge, and by him actions are weighed.

The bows of the mighty men are broken, and they that stumbled are girded with strength.

They that were full have hired out themselves for bread; and they that were hungry ceased: so that the barren hath born seven; and she that hath many children is waxed feeble.

The Lord killeth, and maketh alive: he bringeth down to the grave, and bringeth up.

The Lord maketh poor, and maketh rich: he bringeth low, and lifeth up.

He raiseth up the poor out of the dust, and lifeth up the beggar from the dunghill, to set them among princes, and to make them inherit the throne of glory: for the pillars of the earth are the Lord's, and he hath set the world upon them.

He will keep the feet of his saints, and the wicked shall be silent in darkness; for by strength shall no man prevail.

The adversaries of the Lord shall be broken to pieces; out of heaven shall he thunder upon them: the Lord shall judge the ends of the earth; and he shall give strength unto his king, and exalt the horn of his anointed.

Nehemiah's Prayer

Nehemiah 1:5-11

And said, I beseech thee, O Lord God of heaven,
the great and terrible God, that keepeth covenant
and mercy for them that love him and observe his
commandments:

Let thine ear now be attentive, and thine eyes open,
that thou mayest hear the prayer of thy servant,
which I pray before thee now, day and night, for
the children of Israel thy servants, and confess the
sins of the children of Israel, which we have sinned
against thee: both I and my father's house have
sinned.

We have dealt very corruptly against thee, and have
not kept the commandments, nor the statutes, nor
the judgments, which thou commandest thy servant
Moses.

Remember, I beseech thee, the word that thou
commandedst thy servant Moses saying, if ye trans-
gress, I will scatter You abroad among the nations:

But if ye turn unto me, and keep my commandments,
and do them; though there were of You cast out
unto the uttermost part of the heaven, yet will I
gather them from thence, and will bring them unto
the place that I have chosen to set my name there.

Now these are thy servants and thy people, whom
thou hast redeemed by the great power, and by the
strong hand.

O Lord, I beseech thee, let now thine ear be attentive to the prayer of thy servant, and to the prayer
of thy servants, who desire to fear thy name: and
prosper, I pray thee, thy servant this day, and grant

him mercy in the sight of this man. For I was the king's cupbearer.

Jesus Taught His Disciples How to Pray

Matthew 6:9-13

After this manner therefore pray ye:

Our Father which art in heaven, Hallowed be thy name.

Thy kingdom come. Thy will be done in earth, as it is in heaven.

Give us this day our daily bread.

And forgive us our debts, as we forgive our debtors.

And lead us not into temptation, but deliver us from evil: For thine is the kingdom, and the power, and the glory, for ever. Amen.

The Prayer of Jesus

John 17:1-26

These words spake Jesus, and lifted up his eyes to heaven, and said, Father, the hour is come; glorify thy Son, that the Son also may glorify thee.

As thou hast given him power over all flesh, that he should give eternal life to as many as thou hast given him.

And this is life eternal, that they might know thee the only true God, and Jesus Christ, whom thou hast sent.

I have glorified thee on the earth: I have finished the work which thou gavest me to do.

And now, O Father, glorify thou me with thine own self with the glory which I had with thee before the world was.

I have manifested thy name unto the men which thou gavest me out of the world: thine they were, and thou gavest them me; and they have kept thy word.

Now they have known that all things whatsoever thou has given me are of thee.

For I have given unto them the words which thou gavest me; and they have received them, and have known surely that I came out from thee, and they have believed that thou didst send men.

I pray for them: I pray not for the world, but for them which thou hast given me; for they are thine.

And all mine are thine, and thine are mine; and I am glorified in them.

And now I am no more in the world, but these are in the world, and I come to thee. Holy Father, keep

through thine own name those whom thou hast
given me, that they may be one, as we are.

While I was with them in the world, I kept them in
thy name: those that thou gavest me I have kept,
and none of them is lost, but the son of perdition;
that the scripture might be fulfilled.

And now come I to thee; and these things I speak in
the world, that they might have my joy fulfilled in
themselves.

I have given them thy word; and the world hath hated
them, because they are not of the world, even as I
am not of the world.

I pray not that thou shouldest take them out of the
world, but that thou shouldest keep them from the
evil.

They are not of the world, even as I am not of the
world.

Sanctify them through thy truth: thy word is truth.

As thou hast sent me into the world, even so have I
also sent them into the world.

And for their sakes I sanctify myself, that they also
might be sanctified through the truth.

Neither pray I for these alone, but for them also which
shall believe on me through their word;

That they all may be one; as thou, Father, art in me,
and I in thee, that they also may be one in us: that
the world may believe that thou hast sent me.

And the glory which thou gavest me I have given
them; that they may be one, even as we are one:

I in them, and thou in me, that they may be made
perfect in one; and that the world may know that
thou hast sent me, and hast loved them, as thou hast
loved me.

Father, I will that they also, whom thou hast given me,
be with me where I am; that they may behold my

glory, which thou hast given me: for thou lovedst me before the foundation of the world.

O righteous Father, the world hath not known thee: but I have known thee, and these have known that thou hast sent me.

And I have declared unto them thy name, and will declare it: that the love wherewith thou hast loved me may be in them, and I in them.

The Prayers of Paul

Ephesians 1:16-21

Cease not to give thanks for You, making mention of
   You in my prayers,

That the God of our Lord Jesus Christ, the Father of
   glory, may give unto You the spirit of wisdom and
   revelation in the knowledge of him:

The eyes of Your understanding being enlightened;
   that ye may know what is the hope of his calling,
   and what the riches of the glory of his inheritance
   in the saints,

And what is the exceeding greatness of his power to
   us-ward who believe, according to the working of
   his mighty power,

Which he wrought in Christ when he raised him from
   the dead, and set him at his own right hand in the
   heavenly places,

Far above all principality; and power, and might, and
   dominion, and every name that is named, not only
   in this world but also in that which is to come.

The Prayers of Paul

Ephesians 3:14-21

For this cause I bow my knees unto the Father of our
Lord Jesus Christ,

Of whom the whole family in heaven and earth is
named, according to the riches of his glory, to be
strengthened with might by his Spirit in the inner
man;

That Christ may dwell in Your hearts by faith; that
ye, being rooted and grounded in love,

May be able to comprehend with all saints what is
the breadth, and length, and depth, and height;

And to know the love of Christ, which passeth knowledge, that ye might be filled with all the fullness of
God.

Now unto him that is able to do exceeding abundantly above all that we ask or think, according to
the power that worketh in us,

Unto him be glory in the church by Christ Jesus
throughout all ages, world with end. Amen.

Philippians 1:9-11

And this I pray, that Your love may abound yet more
and more in knowledge and in all judgment;

That ye may approve things that are excellent; that
ye may be sincere and without offence till the day
of Christ;

Being filled with the fruits of righteousness, which
are by Jesus Christ unto the glory and praise of
God.

Colossians 1:9-12

For this cause we also, since the day we heard it, do not cease to pray for You, and to desire that we might be filled with the knowledge of his will in all wisdom and spiritual understanding;

That ye might walk worthy of the Lord unto all pleasing, being fruitful in every good work, and increasing in the knowledge of God;

Strengthened with all might according to his glorious power, unto all patience and longsuffering with joyfulness;

Giving thanks unto the Father, which hath made us meet to be partakers of the inheritance of the saints in light:...

2 Thessalonians 1:11-12

Wherefore also we pray always for You, that our God would count You worthy of this calling, and fulfil all the good pleasure of his goodness, and the work of faith with power:

That the name of our Lord Jesus Christ may be glorified in You, and ye in him, according to the grace of our God and the Lord Jesus Christ.

Chapter 7

Selected Chapters From the Book of Psalms

Psalm 1

Blessed is the man that walketh not in the counsel of the ungodly, nor standeth in the way of sinners, nor sitteth in the seat of the scornful.

But his delight is in the law of the Lord; and in his law doth he meditate day and night.

And he shall be like a tree planted by the rivers of water, that bringeth forth his fruit in his season; his leaf also shall not wither; and whatsoever he doeth shall prosper.

The ungodly are not so: but are like the chaff which the wind driveth away.

Therefore the ungodly shall not stand in the judgment, nor sinners in the congregation of the righteous.

For the Lord knoweth the way of the righteous: but The way of the ungodly shall perish.

Psalm 23

The Lord is my shepherd; I shall not want.

He maketh me to lie down in green pastures: he leadeth me beside the still waters.

He restoreth my soul: he leadeth me in the paths of righteousness for his name's sake.

Yea, though I walk through the valley of the shadow of death, I will fear no evil: for thou art with me; thy rod and thy staff they comfort me.

Thou preparest a table before me in the presence of mine enemies: thou anointest my head with oil; my cup runneth over.

Surely goodness and mercy shall follow me all the days of my life: and I will dwell in the house of the Lord for ever.

Psalm 24

The earth is the Lord's, and the fullness thereof; the world, and they that dwell therein.

For he hath founded it upon the seas, and established it upon the floods.

Who shall ascend into the hill of the Lord? Or who shall stand in his holy place?

He that hath clean hands, and a pure heart; who hath not Lifted up his soul unto vanity, nor sworn deceitfully.

He shall receive the blessing from the Lord, and righteousness from the God of his salvation.

This is the generation of them that seek him, that seek thy face, O Jacob. Selah. lift up Your heads, O ye gates; and be ye lift up, ye everlasting doors; and the King of glory shall come in.

Who is this King of glory? The Lord strong and
mighty, the Lord mighty in battle.

Lift up Your heads, O ye gates; even lift them up,
ye everlasting doors; and the King of glory shall
come in.

Who is this King of glory? The Lord of hosts, he is
the King of glory. Selah.

Psalm 67

God be merciful unto us, and bless us; and cause his
face to shine upon us. Selah.

That they way may be known upon earth, thy saving
health among all nations.

Let the people praise thee, O God; let all the people
praise thee.

O let the nations be glad and sing for joy: for thou
shalt judge the people righteously, and govern the
nations upon earth. Selah.

Let the people praise thee, O God; let all the people
praise thee.

Then shall the earth yield her increase; and God, even
our own God, shall bless us.

God shall bless us; and all the ends of the earth shall
fear him.

Psalm 70

Make haste, O God, to deliver me; make haste to
help me, O Lord.

Let them be ashamed and confounded that seek after
my soul: let them be turned backward, and put to
confusion, that desire my hurt.

Let them be turned back for a reward of their shame that say, Aha, aha.

Let all those that seek thee rejoice and be glad in thee: and let such as love thy salvation say continually, Let God be magnified.

But I am poor and needy: make haste unto me, O God: thou art my help and my deliverer; O Lord, make no tarrying.

Psalm 100

Make a joyful noise unto the Lord, all ye lands.

Serve the Lord with gladness: come before his presence with singing.

Know ye that the Lord he is God: it is he that hath made us, and not we ourselves; we are his people, and the sheep of his pasture.

Enter into his gates with thanksgiving, and into his courts with praise: be thankful unto him, and bless his name.

For the Lord is good; his mercy is everlasting; and his truth endureth to all generations.

Psalm 117

O praise the Lord, all ye nations: praise him, all ye people.

For his merciful kindness is great toward us: and the truth of the Lord endureth for ever. Praise ye the Lord.

Psalm 121

I will lift up mine eyes unto the hills, from whence cometh my help.

My help cometh from the Lord, which made heaven and earth.

He will not suffer thy foot to be moved: he that keepeth thee will not slumber.

Behold, he that keepeth Israel shall neither slumber nor sleep.

The Lord is thy keeper: the Lord is thy shade upon thy right hand.

The sun shall not smite thee by day, nor the moon by night.

The Lord shall preserve thee from all evil: he shall preserve thy soul.

The Lord shall preserve thy going out and thy coming in from this time forth, and even for evermore.

Psalm 125

They that trust in the Lord shall be as mount Zion, which cannot be removed, but abideth for ever.

As the mountains are round about Jerusalem, so the Lord is round about his people from henceforth even for ever.

For the rod of the wicked shall not rest upon the lot of the righteous; lest the righteous put forth their hands unto iniquity.

Do good, O Lord, unto those that be good, and to them that are upright in their hearts.

As for such as turn aside unto their crooked ways, the Lord shall lead them forth with the workers of iniquity: but peace shall be upon Israel.

Psalm 133

Behold, how good and how pleasant it is for brethren
to dwell together in unity!
It is like the precious ointment upon the head, that
ran down upon the beard, even Aaron's beard: that
went down to the skirts of his garments;
As the dew of Hermon, and as the dew that
descended upon the mountains of Zion: for there
the Lord commanded the blessing, even life for
evermore.

Psalm 134

Behold, bless ye the Lord, all ye servants of the Lord,
which by night stand in the house of the Lord.
Lift up Your hands in the sanctuary, and bless the
Lord.
The Lord that made heaven and earth bless thee out
of Zion.

Psalm 150

Praise ye the Lord. Praise God in his sanctuary: praise
him in the firmament of his power.
Praise him for his mighty acts: praise him according
to his excellent greatness.
Praise him with the sound of the trumpet: praise him
with psaltery and harp.
Praise him with the timbrel and dance: praise him
with stringed instruments and organs.
Praise him upon the loud cymbals: praise him upon
the high sounding cymbals.

Let every thing that hath breath praise the Lord. Praise ye the Lord.

Chapter 8

Affirm His Name

In the Book of Psalms Chapter 8 verse 1 declares, *"O Lord our Lord, how excellent is thy name in all the earth! Who hast set thy glory above the heavens."* His name is excellent. Call upon His name. He will reveal His provisions made for You through the power of his names. Be enriched as You affirm His name.

1. The Lord is my Jehovah-Jireh (The Lord is my Provider) (Genesis 22:8, 14).

2. The Lord is my Jehovah-Rapha (The Lord is my Healer) (Exodus 15:26).

3. The Lord is my Jehovah-Nissi (The Lord is my Banner) (Exodus 17:15).

4. The Lord is my Jehovah-Makaddish (The Lord is my Sanctifier) (Leviticus 20:7-8).

5. The Lord is my Jehovah-Shalom (The Lord is my Peace) (Judges 6:24).

6. The Lord is my Jehovah-Tsidkenu (The Lord is my Righteousness) (Jeremiah 23:5-6).

7. The Lord is my Jehovah-Shammah (The Lord is There) (Ezekiel 48:35).

8. The Lord is my Jehovah-Rohi (The Lord is my Shepherd) (Psalms 23:1).

Chapter 9

Fourteen Ways to Maintain Heavenly Joy

1. Spend time in the Word of God (Proverbs 3:13).
2. Pray (Luke 18:1).
3. Have Faith (Mark 11:22).
4. Talk Faith (Romans 10:10; St. Matthew 7:7-8).
5. Think on Good Things (Philippians 4:8).
6. Go to Church (Psalm 122:1).
7. Praise the Lord (Psalm 150).
8. Give (St. Luke 6:38; II Corinthians 9:7).
9. Expect the Best (Jeremiah 29:11).
10. Forgive (Mark 11:25).
11. Eat Healthy (Mark 6:37; I Timothy 4:4-5).
12. Exercise (I Timothy 4:8).
13. Communicate with Positive People (I Corinthians 15:33; Proverbs 13:20; Ephesians 4:29).
14. Count Your Blessings (Proverbs 28:20).

Chapter 10

Steps to Financial Freedom

A few years ago, I was swamped in credit card debt. I owed my whole paycheck to creditors. I was living from paycheck to paycheck and borrowing money in between. I was on my way to file bankruptcy. The Spirit of the Lord spoke to me and showed me a better way to come out of debt and into financial freedom. I would like to share the plan that worked for me to get out of debt.

1. Sit down with pen and paper.
2. Make a list of everyone you owe.
3. Create a plan/budget to come out of debt.
4. Give Tithes and offerings (Malachi 3:8-10, Hebrews 7:2).
5. Save 1%, 2% of your income for yourself.
6. Increase savings as You become free of debt.
7. Make arrangements with creditors to pay bills.
8. Ask creditor to lower interest rate. Ask again. They may do this.
9. Regularly make the agreed payment each month.
10. Set deadline for each bill to be paid off.
11. Pay smallest bills off first.
12. Review your plan daily.

13. Stop impulse buying.
14. Stop using credit cards.
15. Make a list before shopping. Stick to Your list.
16. Cook at home. Eat out less.
17. Prepare lunch for work.
18. Fill up Your gas tank. The gas tends to last longer.
19. Live on cash basis.
20. Avoid borrowing money.

Once again, this plan delivered me from the bondage of debt. God wants You debt-free. Read the Word to know the truth concerning financial freedom. *". . . ye shall know the truth, and the truth shall make You free" (John 8:32).* Confess debt freedom. By acting on your confession, you are well on your way to a debt-free lifestyle.

Don't allow the spirit of debt to drag you back into bondage. Acknowledge God in all your ways, His supernatural power will help you live in financial freedom. Read these scriptures concerning financial freedom: 2 Kings 4:1-7, Jeremiah 32:17, Proverbs, and Matthew 21:21, Matthew 17:25-27, Hebrews 13:8, and Acts 10:34.

Chapter 11

101 Pleasant Words

Pleasant words are as a honeycomb, sweet to the
soul, and health to the bones.
Proverbs 16:24

Refresh Your soul and the soul of other people by speaking pleasant words. The scripture says pleasant words are sweet to the soul and health to the bones. Speaking pleasant words enables one to live a healthy and joyful life.

A pleasant word motivates an infant to smile; an old person to dance; a student to excel to the top of the class. A pleasant word motivates a wife to cook the best meal; and a husband to walk in confidence among his peers.

Pleasant words spoken to people will come back to You. Words are powerful and can tear down or build up. Words can hurt or can heal. Let us speak words that will build and heal.

Here is a list of everyday, down to earth, pleasant words:

1. Hello!
2. God loves You.
3. I like Your positive attitude.

4. Great job.
5. Outstanding.
6. I love You.
7. You are a good man.
8. You are handsome.
9. You are a jewel.
10. I am proud of You.
11. Keep up the good work.
12. You look confident.
13. I like Your posture.
14. Your idea is great.
15. You are weird in a good way.
16. I believe in You.
17. I have something for You.
18. You are beautiful.
19. You have a great sense of humor.
20. You smell nice.
21. You are cool.
22. I miss You.
23. What can I do for You?
24. You make me feel good.
25. What do You think?
26. You are right.
27. You will do just fine.
28. You are strong.
29. God bless You.
30. It is nice to meet You.
31. Welcome back.
32. You got it going on.
33. You are a winner.
34. You are the best!
35. You make smart choices.
36. Live strong.
37. Peace.
38. You are welcome.

39. I will pray for You.
40. You are friendly.
41. You are kind.
42. You are thoughtful.
43. You are generous.
44. Those grades are wonderful.
45. Do You need help?
46. Thank You for helping me with this or that.
47. I appreciate the help You have given me.
48. You can do it!
49. Good work!
50. You look like Your Mom.
51. Just try and do Your best.
52. You will get it next time.
53. I will be glad to help You.
54. I am here for You.
55. Keep going. You are doing well.
56. You have nice clothes.
57. I like Your hair.
58. I like Your shoes.
59. I like Your smile.
60. I like Your laughter.
61. You are very good in sports.
62. Super!
63. Goodbye. See You tomorrow.
64. I will stand with You.
65. You are not alone.
66. I will call You.
67. You have a beautiful smile.
68. You are going somewhere.
69. What's Your name?
70. The best is coming Your way.
71. Thanks for Your patience.
72. You make me happy.
73. You are courageous.

74. I like Your style.
75. Yes.
76. Excuse me.
77. Please.
78. Thank You.
79. You are positive.
80. You are the best Dad.
81. You are the best Mom.
82. I thought what You did was great.
83. You are going to the top.
84. I trust You.
85. I feel happy when You look at me and smile.
86. You always smell really nice.
87. You are a great kid!
88. You are my best friend.
89. You are such a good friend.
90. You are intelligent.
91. You have made my day.
92. Thanks for listening.
93. You always seem to find a way to make me smile.
94. Let us spend time together.
95. I like to hear You laugh.
96. I like to see You smile.
97. I love the way You walk.
98. You are fun to be around.
99. Happy Birthday!
100. I appreciate You.
101. Congratulations!

To contact Mary E. Scott Mayo, write:

Pastor Mary E. Scott Mayo
Joy and Deliverance Christian Church
P. O. Box 25442
Raleigh, NC 27611

Phone: 919.828.8822 or 919.231.3393

If You would like to make a contribution to this ministry,
please send it to the above address.
Your contributions are greatly appreciated.

About the Author

❋

Pastor Mary Elizabeth Scott Mayo was born and raised in Raleigh, North Carolina. After graduating from West Cary High School, she obtained a Bachelor of Arts degree in Business Education from Saint Augustine's College, Raleigh, North Carolina. She began her professional career with North Carolina State University as a Stenographer IV. From several jobs in between, she became an administrator at IBM, Research Triangle Park, North Carolina.

Pastor Mayo is the Founder and Senior Pastor of Joy and Deliverance Christian Church in Raleigh, North Carolina. She has served since June 1995.

Pastor Mayo is blessed to have her husband, Clarence Mayo, Jr., their children and grandchildren working in the ministry.

To the Point, Down to Earth, Scriptures, Affirmations and Prayers to Put Heaven into Your Day and Kick Hell Out!

Heaven is not automatic…You need preparation to get there. Start today by speaking Spirit-filled words to put You into heavenly places. *"And hath raised us up together, and made us sit together in heavenly places in Christ Jesus: that in the ages to come he might shew the exceeding riches of his grace in his kindness toward us through Christ Jesus (Ephesians 2:6-7).*

Put heaven into Your day as You speak the scriptures, affirm, and pray the Word of God. You can be confident that You are praying in line with God's will and that He will honor His Word. Take hold of the Word and kick hell (destruction, fear, worry, torment, and confusion) out. Allow God to work on Your behalf as You pray for these topics:

❈ Family
❈ Health
❈ Business
❈ Prosperity
❈ Plus many more!

"That Your days may be multiplied, and the days of Your children, in the land which the Lord swear unto Your fathers to give them, as the days of heaven upon the earth" (Deuteronomy 11:21).

Printed in the United States
200118BV00006B/19-45/A

9 781604 770759